How To Get Answers Every Time You pray

Using Your Voice

Tiffany L. Long

Based on the original book, "How To Get Answers Every Time You Pray, The Power Of Partnership" © Copyright 2005 Dr. Ludie L. Hoffman

Revision Created:

"HOW TO GET ANSWERS EVERYTIME YOU PRAY: USING YOUR VOICE"

©Copyright 2020 Tiffany Long

Interfaith University Press-

All rights reserved

In partnership with AMC Consultants

It is not legal to reproduce, duplicate, or transmit any part of this document in either electronic means or printed format, recording of this publication is strictly prohibited.

Table of Contents

Chapter One: The Power of Your Voice   1

Chapter Two: What Is Agreement?   8

Chapter Three: Prayer   14

Chapter Four: What is IT?   17

Chapter Five: God's Will   31

Chapter Six: Covenants   32

Chapter Seven: Impartation   41

Chapter Eight: A Prayer for Our Government   49

Chapter Nine: A Prayer for Our Schools   54

Chapter 10: A Prayer for Revival   60

Chapter 11: Understanding Redemption   72

Chapter 12: Understanding Confession   82

Chapter 13: Your Opportunity to Partners   88

Chapter 14: The Blessing of The Twice Sown seed   91

Chapter 15: Prayer for Our Ministry Partner   100

Acknowledgments

Thank you Apostle Dr. Ludie Hoffman for allowing me the opportunity to revise and expound further on his How To Get Answers Every Time You Pray: The Power Of Partnership Copyright © 2005 book. Dr. L. Hoffman has allowed me to share with individuals how they can use their voice to change their life for the better. In this book individuals will learn how they can open their mouth and declare God's word over their circumstances and watch it turn around for the better.

Dr. Ludie L. Hoffman is the originator of the "How to Get answers Every Time You Pray: The Power Of Partnership Copyright © 2005". "How to Get Answers Every Time You Pray: Using Your Voice is a revision of what has been written by Dr. Ludie L. Hoffman.

Chapter One:

The Power of Using Your Voice

The bible says in Proverbs 18:21 that Life and death are in the power of the tongue, and they that love it shall eat the fruit thereof. The amplified translation says it like this, "Death and life are in the power of the tongue, And those who love it and indulge it will eat its fruit and bear the consequences of their words". God has given each of us a voice. We can see from the verse stated above that each human voice has power.

It can literally make a difference whether people see life or death in their lives. It can make a difference whether a person accomplishes their goals or not. It can be so easy to speak negativity nowadays. In the world today, bad means good and good means bad. A good example would be the saying, "I laughed my self to death". Just take a moment and think about what you're saying. Do you really want to laugh until you're dead? Is that something that you want to really experience in your life? This can happen so many times in our lives, speaking things in our lives that we don't want to experience, and then we wonder why we are having some of the challenges we face. It's because of what we're saying.

Ezekiel 37 verse 1-14 says, **The hand of the Lord was upon me, and carried me out in the spirit of the Lord, and set me down in the midst of the valley which was full of bones, 2 And caused me to pass by them round about: and, behold, there were very many in the open valley; and, lo, they were very dry. 3 And he said unto me, Son of man, can these bones live? And I answered, O Lord God, thou knowest. 4 Again he said unto me, Prophesy upon these bones, and say unto them, O ye dry bones, hear the word of the Lord. 5 Thus saith the Lord God unto these bones; Behold, I will cause breath to enter into you, and ye shall live: 6 And I will lay** sinews upon you, and will bring up flesh upon you, and cover you with skin, and put breath in you, and ye shall live; and ye shall know that I am the Lord. 7 So I prophesied as I was commanded: and as I prophesied, there was a noise, and behold a shaking, and the bones came together, bone to his bone. 8 And when I beheld, lo, the sinews and the flesh came up upon them, and the skin covered them above: but there was no breath in them. 9 Then said he unto me, Prophesy unto the wind, prophesy, son of man, and say to the wind, Thus saith the Lord God; Come from the four winds, O breath, and breathe upon these slain, that they may live. 10 So I prophesied as he commanded me, and the breath came into them, and they lived, and stood up upon their feet, an exceeding great army. 11 Then he said unto me, Son of man, these bones are the whole house of Israel: behold, they say, Our bones are dried, and our hope is lost: we are cut off for our parts. 12 Therefore prophesy and say unto them, Thus saith the Lord God; Behold, O my people, I will open your graves, and cause you to come up out of your graves, and bring you into the land of Israel. 13 And ye shall know that I am the Lord, when I have opened your graves, O my people, and brought you up out of your graves, 14 And shall put my spirit in you,

and ye shall live, and I shall place you in your own land: then shall ye know that I the Lord have spoken it, and performed it, saith the Lord.

Here we can see in Ezekiel 37 that our voice has power. It can turn a situation that seemed to be bad around for the good. If we want to experience this in our life. First, we must realize that our words have power, then we must only speak those words that build up and not tear down. Some may be asking, well how do I do that, you simply speak only what God says on the situation, and you can find what God says on any situation that you may be going through in His word, through the bible.

Search the scriptures and find out what God says about the situation and begin to confess those things instead.

Chapter Two:
What is Agreement?

Verily I say unto you, Whatsoever ye shall bind on earth shall be bound in heaven: and whatsoever ye shall loose on earth shall be loosed in heaven. 19 Again I say unto you, that if two of you shall agree on earth as touching anything that they shall ask, it shall be done for them of my Father which is in heaven. Matthew 18:18-19

Can two walk together, except they be agreed? Amos 3:3

To agree comes from a Greek word sumphoneo, from sum-together and phoneo- to sound. The word Sumphoneo means to sound together, to be in symphony, to be in accord, to be in harmony. Metaphorically, the word means to agree together in prayer. Matthew 18:19-19 talks about the power that the church must call on heaven. Let's take a closer look at Matthew 18:18, whatsoever you bind, whatsoever you loose, heaven will agree, this is scripturally based. This is the power that the church has, when they pray, results are manifested. This is one of the many benefits that we have because of the sacrifice of Christ.

The bible is constantly reminding us of the many benefits that we have in Christ Jesus, it says to forget not all His benefits. The results of a survey said that 80% of individuals who are in the church who are called to be like God (our Father who is in heaven) are yet dying- spiritually, physically, mentally, socially, and even financially. It is a must that we go back and reexamine the definition of the word "saved. What are we saved from? Sin? If sin is no longer a part of our life, then we need to realize that God doesn't save us halfway. Christ literally died to make us completely whole. This includes our body, soul, and our spirit. Christ came to heal those who were brokenhearted, not just fix one part of their life, and leave the rest undone, but it is our Father's desire that we be made completely whole.

It is important to remember that Satan's job is to control you by unbelief in the atonement of Christ. This is why 80% of individuals don't pray because they don't see the use in disciplining themselves to commune with a God that doesn't have provision for them. This is the reason for the subconscious hearts of the 80% of those who approach God through attending church services don't experience the full manifestation of the blessings that God has freely and fully laid out for us. Thus, we can't agree on what God says, for many times we don't know.

God's people aren't destroyed because Satan is so much more powerful than them, or because they are broken, afflicted, or ragged. The bible says in Hosea 4:6 that they are destroyed because a lack of knowledge. Now is the time that we learn of the many benefits of salvation, in the fullness that the scriptures lay out for us. Let's begin to pray and give like never before, until our prayers reach to heaven and build a memorial before our Father like Cornelius did.

Then God can connect us with a Peter that has prepared himself through prayer for the glory of God. Next there will be an exchange of the anointing and power of God that will fall on us just like the Holy Ghost fell on Cornelius and his house. The miracles and benefits we often read about will become a reality in our life. Read more in Acts Chapter 10.

Chapter Three:

Prayer

Let's take a look at the definition of the word prayer before we go further. Pray is explained by Jesus by the Greek prosseuchomai _pros-yoo-khom-ahee). The word prosseuchomai is a progressive word starting with the noun euche, this is prayer to God that includes making a vow.

The word expands out to the verb euchomai, it's a special term describing " an invocation, request or entreaty". Adding pros, in the direction of God, prossechomai becomes most frequent word used for prayer.

Looking at the meaning here, invocation is where the power of agreement can be found. In Genesis 11, the unity that the people had together caused God to take notice of what they were doing at the Tower of Babel. He came down to stop the work and confuse their languages. The translation here is unity at work, brings God's presence on the scene. Let's look at it from the positive. On the Day of Pentecost, they were all together with one accord and God came down again. (Acts Chapter 2). Unity at work that is directed towards God whether it's negative or positive will get God's attention. If you are born again, you have unity, you have the measure of unity that brings us into God's family. This is where we must get into the word of God and learn how to work that unity for positive and productive reasons that God has given us. Unity cannot be left alone; it needs to be activated in the direction towards God.

Chapter Four:

What is IT?

Let's talk about It. A reason many Christians who pray don't have what they pray for is the IT. Many pray for the IT and IT doesn't come, why is this? Because IT must in unity with a person on earth, but it has to be loosed from heaven too. This following process will get you anything you desire. Philippians 4:19 says, "But my God shall supply all your need according to his riches in glory by Christ Jesus", want (Psalms 23:1-6), **23** The Lord is my shepherd; I shall not want. ² He maketh me to lie down in green pastures: he leadeth me beside the still waters. ³ He restoreth my soul: he leadeth me in the paths of righteousness for his name's sake. ⁴ Yea, though I walk through the valley of the shadow of death, I will fear no evil: for thou art with me; thy rod and thy staff they comfort me. ⁵ Thou preparest a table before me in the presence of mine enemies: thou anointest my head with oil; my cup runneth over. ⁶ Surely goodness and mercy shall follow me all the days of my life: and I will dwell in the house of the Lord for ever.

or desire from God Psalms 37:4 says, "Delight thyself also in the Lord; and he shall give thee the desires of thine heart.

1. Analyze the situation- Find out what your needs are, what your debts are, what your sickness is, or what the fear is about. Find out how much of what it is you need in order to sustain yourself, for your family, and for the House of God. The bible says that in 2 Corinthians 13:5 that 5 Examine yourselves, whether ye be in the faith; prove your own selves. Know ye not your own selves, how that Jesus Christ is in you, except ye be reprobates? This simply means that we must examine ourselves when we're asking of God to make sure were not asking amiss.

2. Research God's Remedy- Just like we would ask our doctor what medication is right for a specific problem, don't forget to ask our great Physician. Ask God to show us in His word what the cure is for our specific situation. We must remember to ask God for His perspective on the situation. Next search and research the bible until you have allowed the Holy Spirit to convince you of the truth that Christ has redeemed you from the curse of the law, as stated in Galatians 3:13.
3. Ask, Seek, Knock- This is the next step, once you know what the will of God is, which is based on scripture, this is not

based on a prophet or any other person, but it is found in the Word of God. Then He will hasten his Word to perform it as Matthew 7:7 states. What this means is that it takes consistently being persistent and growing in intensity and faith until our Father gets up and grants your request.

4. Partner- You may be thinking, I've done the stated above step, I ask, I seek, and I knock, but I still haven't gotten my breakthrough. The next step is you MUST partner. When you're at your faith limit, remember that you're never alone. There are other saints that have been down the road that you are trying to

embark on. There are other saints that have had the same challenges that you are trying to overcome, and you have access to their faith through the power of agreement. James 5: 14-16. Verse 14 says, Is any sick among you? let him call for the elders of the church; and let them pray over him, anointing him with oil in the name of the Lord. Pay close attention to " call for the Elders of the church". There are two principles that are stated here that never needs to be ignored.

1. Elder- Simply means older, it doesn't always mean in age, but speaking to maturity in the Lord. An elder at the

least is mature in the area that you are weak in. Disclaimer: if you are having problems or a weakness, a prayer partner with the same struggle is not going to build you up; they aren't developed themselves to the point where they can handle their infirmity and yours, instead of agreeing with God you begin to unite against God and a tower is starting to form, a tower of confusion.

2. Never forget that the binding and loosing power is connected to the Church. Make it your rule to never partner with someone who is not rooted and grounded in a local

church. (When it deals with your deliverance.) It is okay to pray with someone who is not in a local church, who understands that the focus of the prayer is for their edification mostly. However, if you need strength, you need to find strong prayer partners as Matthew 18:18-19 speaks on. Maybe you have a prayer partner and still have a problem, start at the end of the steps and if all lines are clear, bring in another prayer partner and another one until you have enough power in prayer to bind the strong man or the negative force that is blocking your flow of blessing. Make sure all your prayer partners understand and has done the things stated above and can agree with you that this IT is the will of God. and he wants you to have IT. start building your prayer partnership today.

5. Begin to Start praising and worshiping God in Faith and watch Him manifest it.

6. Separate yourself from bad company. negative friends, bad teaching and preaching that is not in faith in God's Word (I Corinthians 15:33), Be not deceived: evil communications corrupt good manners.

7. If the enemy try's to attack you with thoughts of doubt- do it again (Galatians 6:6).

The bottom line of your IT must be in line with your prayer partners level of faith and the will of the Father in Heaven. Some may wonder, how do we know the will of the Father? We must know, agree, and pray in accordance to the Word of our Father in heaven. If God says IT, we can count on it, and agree with God. We must say what God says and you will truly have whatsoever you say. What is your IT? Matthew 6:33 talks about seeking first the righteousness of God and he will commence to dropping it on you. How do we seek the kingdom of God?

1. Look for and pray for opportunities to sow- your finances, time, energy, and prayer into a ministry that is anointed and that is spreading the gospel of Christ. A ministry that has vision.

2. Preach the Word- witness to your friends and neighbors. Give away good sound Christian books, MP3 downloads and videos. Find ways to get the gospel out in any way you can in the Spirit of God. (Pray about it!)

3. Put God first- Stop thinking of how much God can do for you and think about

how much you can do for the kingdom of God. It may take only a little car for you to live, but the kingdom of God may call for a minivan to help people get to church, pray until you find out what God wants you to have because that is your need. You may be fine in a one-bedroom apartment, but a Christian brother or sister may need help some, and the kingdom of God may be calling for a four-bedroom home. Seek the kingdom of God and His righteousness. It's time to get the IT right because when you hunger and thirst to help and reach out to others, you will be super blessed over and over. This doesn't mean we run off and sow financial seed to everything asking that looks like the kingdom of God? No! Would you sow one or two peas to a field? No! Because in that case, you would have to go to different locations to get a pot started. The bottom line is to sow where:

1. Where God leads you

2. Where the ground is good

3. Where the Gospel is being preached

4. Where souls are being saved

5. Where Christian's are edified

All these things should be done under of the witness of the Holy Spirit. Pray, God will direct your steps. What is IT? Let's touch and agree and it is done according to God's will.

Chapter Five:

God's Will

We have already talked about that God's word is His will. Let's dig deeper. If you want to experience the true blessing of God, you must allow God to speak to your heart about your need and back it up with scripture. You must make that scripture and revealed word of God your faith. That's true, the moment God makes a word alive in your spirit you have faith, now. Hebrews 11:1 says, Now faith is the substance of things hoped for, the evidence of things not seen. Romans 10:17 says, faith comes by hearing and hearing by the Word of God.

Chapter Six:

Covenants

From the beginning of time God has been revealed as the covenant maker. A simple meaning of the word "covenant" in the bible is summed up by the book of Jeremiah chapter 31 verse 33: "I will be their God; and they will be my people." God begins a special relationship with men and women. He commits himself to protect them, and in return he expects obedience from them. Most of the covenants in the bible are between God and man. "Man to man" covenants can also be seen in the Old Testament in the bible. The bible is divided into two big covenants, the old and the new. More often are they called the Old and the New Testament (which means the same thing). The old covenant can be seen with Moses on Mt. Sinai, when the ten commandments were given to the people of God as basic rules for them to live by. This covenant forms the basis for Israel's religion.

Other covenants in the Old Testament can be seen. God made a covenant with Noah after the flood. This is God's general covenant with all people. He also made a covenant with Abraham. God promised his descendants that they would have a land of their own and encouraged them to share that blessing with other nations of the earth. This is the covenant of God with His special people. It is renewed with Moses at Mt. Sinai.

In the New Testament writers begin to show the new covenant between God and men to which the Old Testament looks forward, and rest on the death of Jesus. Jesus said Himself " this cup of the new covenant, sealed with My blood." The book of Hebrews compares the old and the new covenants. The new covenant offers the people of God something that the old could never secure- release from the power of sin, and a new freedom to obey to God.

Exodus 19:6 And ye shall be unto me a kingdom of priests, and an holy nation. These are the words which thou shalt speak unto the children of Israel.

Exodus 20:1-7 And God spake all these words, saying, ² I am the Lord thy God, which have brought thee out of the land of Egypt, out of the house of bondage. ³ Thou shalt have no other gods before me. ⁴ Thou shalt not make unto thee any graven image, or any likeness of anything that is in heaven above, or that is in the earth beneath, or that is in the water under the earth. ⁵ Thou shalt not bow down thyself to them, nor serve them: for I the Lord thy God am a jealous God, visiting the iniquity of the fathers upon the children unto the third and fourth generation of them that hate me; ⁶ And shewing mercy unto thousands of them that love me, and keep my commandments. ⁷ Thou shalt not take the name of the Lord thy God in vain; for the Lord will not hold him guiltless that taketh his name in vain.

Hebrews 8:13 In that he saith, A new covenant, he hath made the first old. Now that which decayeth and waxeth old is ready to vanish away.

Hebrews 10:4 For it is not possible that the blood of bulls and of goats should take away sins.

1 Corinthians 11:25 After the same manner also he took the cup, when he had supped, saying, this cup is the New Testament

in my blood: this do ye, as oft as ye drink it, in remembrance of me

Genesis 9:1-17

Genesis 12:1-3

12 Now the Lord had said unto Abram, Get thee out of thy country, and from thy kindred, and from thy father's house, unto a land that I will shew thee: 2 And I will make of thee a great nation, and I will bless thee, and make thy name great; and thou shalt be a blessing: 3 And I will bless them that bless thee, and curse him that curseth thee: and in thee shall all families of the earth be blessed.

Genesis 15:17-21

17 And it came to pass, that, when the sun went down, and it was dark, behold a smoking furnace, and a burning lamp that passed between those pieces. 18 In the same day the Lord made a covenant with Abram, saying, Unto thy seed have I given this land, from the river of Egypt unto the great river, the river Euphrates: 19 The Kenites, and the Kenizzites, and the Kadmonites, 20 And the Hittites, and the Perizzites, and the Rephaims, 21 And the Amorites, and the Canaanites, and the Girgashites, and the Jebusites.

Jeremiah 31:31-34.

31 Behold, the days come, saith the Lord, that I will make a new covenant with the house

of Israel, and with the house of Judah: 32 Not according to the covenant that I made with their fathers in the day that I took them by the hand to bring them out of the land of Egypt; which my covenant they brake, although I was an husband unto them, saith the Lord: 33 But this shall be the covenant that I will make with the house of Israel; After those days, saith the Lord, I will put my law in their inward parts, and write it in their hearts; and will be their God, and they shall be my people. 34 And they shall teach no more every man his neighbour, and every man his brother, saying, Know the Lord: for they shall all know me, from the least of them unto the greatest of them, saith the Lord:

for I will forgive their iniquity, and I will remember their sin no more.

Chapter Seven:
Impartation

Through the new covenant we can see a new revelation of who God is and how we not only seek the kingdom of God and His righteousness, but in the BLOOD, we find IT.

Our example prayer says, "Thy will be done on earth, as it is in heaven." Translation: The will of God is to bring heaven to earth and to fulfill that, He makes covenant with man. When those who have a covenant with God get together, they make up the body of Christ, the church, and they bring the kingdom of God on earth.

"Now it came about when he had finished talking to Saul, that the soul of David and

Jonathan were knit together and he loved him as himself. And Saul took him that day and did not let him return to his father's house. Then Jonathan made a covenant with David because he loved him as himself. And Jonathan stripped himself of the robe that was on him and gave it to David, with his armor, including his sword and his bow and his belt (1 Samuel 18:14 NASV).

What a covenant between two God fearing men. They became unified in such a way and agreed to the point that Jonathan let down his defense and joined himself to David. He took his armor off and opened himself up to receive whatever David would return to him. David returned with love. The armor was the token of exchange, this can be seen among covenant makers in the bible. God provides protection and provision and in return we are to respond in loving obedience to Him. Jonathan gave to David his royal robe, his armor and sword, his bow and belt, this was Jonathan's way of giving his authority of succession to his father's throne.

To impart simply means to give, share, distribute, grant. The implication of the word is liberality or generosity. It is used to encourage those with two outer tunics to give one to someone who doesn't have. (Luke 3:11 He answereth and saith unto them, He that hath two coats, let him impart to him that hath none;

and he that hath meat, let him do likewise.); to encourage people to give with cheerful outflow (Romans 12:8 Or he that exhorteth, on exhortation: he that giveth, let him do it with simplicity; he that ruleth, with diligence; he that sheweth mercy, with cheerfulness.); and to urge workers to labor with industry, in order to give to him who has a need (Ephesians 4:28 Let him that stole steal no more: but rather let him labour, working with his hands the thing which is good, that he may have to give to him that needeth.).

Ephesians 4:7-8 says, "But unto every one of us is given grace according to the measure of the gift of Christ. Wherefore he saith, when he ascended up on high, he led captivity captive, and gave gifts unto men." Therefore, every Christian has a gift in God. Verse (12) says, "...for the work of the ministry, for the edifying of the Body of Christ."

Paul wrote to the church at Rome and said "For I long to see you, that I may impart unto you some spiritual gift, to the end that ye may be established" (Romans 1:11). To impart here means to " to give over and to share". It means to convey from one person to another. The Apostle Paul had a desire to impart to the saints some spiritual gifts or spiritual help.

Spiritual impartations are given to us to help us complete the will of God for our lives.

This is a part of our equipping process. Through impartation we are equipped to do the work of the ministry.

As a result, establishment happens. The New English Bible says, "to make you strong."

The Twentieth Century New Testament says, "and so give you fresh strength." Thus the believer is equipped with fresh strength as a result of impartation.

Impartation will come many times through association. In this way, there will be a transference of the anointing from or to the people you associate with. We can receive through impartation from the ministries that we submit to and associate with.

There are certain people whom I believe the Lord has destined you to hook up with in the Spirit. They will have the spiritual deposits that you need. God desires that we have all the necessary gifts, information, materials, or anointing (in manifestation of the Holy Spirit). He has given us the path to obtain all we need. He is always ready and willing to equip us with all the grace we need to complete our commission which is to preach the gospel to all the nations and to make disciples of men.

If we are lacking anything, it's not God's fault. It is important to associate with churches and ministries that are strong. If you are associated with something that is weak, then you will become weak. If you associate yourself with strength, then you will become strong. You will become like the people you associate with. Don't allow yourself to become weak by linking up with the wrong type of people. "And God wrought special miracles by the hands of Paul; so that from his body were brought unto the sick handkerchiefs or aprons, and the disease departed from them, and evil spirits went out of them" (Acts 19:11-12). Once again, an object was exchanged (Paul's materials), this is a point of contact (tokens of covenant) to the other person who was a part of the impartation.

Chapter Eight:

A Prayer for Our Government

I Timothy 2:1-2 says that we are to pray, intercede and give thanks for the kings and all people in authority. This is God's command to every believer today. Here is a confession for you to use in prayer for our nation and its leaders. Pray it in faith, believing, and remember God watches over His Word to perform it. (Jeremiah 1:12, The Amplified Bible)

"Father, in Jesus' Name, I give thanks for our country and its government. I bring before You the men and women in positions of authority. I pray and intercede for the president, congressmen, senators, judges, policemen, governors, mayors of our land.

I pray for all people in authority over us in any way.

I pray that the Spirit of the Lord rests upon them. I believe that skillful and godly wisdom has entered into the heart of our president and knowledge is pleasant to him. Discretion watches over him; understanding keeps him and delivers him from the way of evil and from evil men.

Father, I ask You to encompass the president with men and women who make their hearts and ears attentive to godly counsel and who do that which is right in Your sight.

I believe you cause them to be men and women of integrity, who are obedient concerning us. I believe that they lead us in a quiet and peaceable life in all godliness and honesty.

Your Word declares, "Blessed is the nation whose God is the Lord. I receive your Blessing and declare with my mouth that Your people dwell safely in this land, and they prosper abundantly.

It is written in Your Word that the heart of the king is in the hand of the Lord and that You turn it whichever way You desire. I believe the heart of our leader is in Your hand and that his decisions are divinely directed of the Lord. I give thanks unto You that the good news of the gospel is published in our land. The Word of the Lord prevails and grows mightily in the hearts and lives of the people. I give thanks for this land and the leaders you have given to us, in Jesus' Name. I proclaim that Jesus is LORD over the United States of America!

Prayer Reference:

I Timothy 2:1-2

2 I exhort therefore, that, first of all, supplications, prayers, intercessions, and giving of thanks, be made for all men; 2 For kings, and for all that are in authority; that we may lead a quiet and peaceable life in all godliness and honesty.

Proverbs 2:11-12, The Amplified Bible:

11 Discretion will watch over you,

Understanding and discernment will guard you,

12 To keep you from the way of evil and the evil man,

From the man who speaks perverse things;

  Psalms 33:12; 21

Psalms 33:12 Blessed is the nation whose God is the Lord; and the people whom he hath chosen for his own inheritance.

Psalms 33:21 For our heart shall rejoice in him, because we have trusted in his holy name.

Chapter Nine:
A Prayer for Our Schools

More than 44 million students are enrolled in the United States' public schools.

They are instructed by 2.6 million teachers. These numbers certainly justify a tremendous spiritual outreach and call to intercessory prayer. What are we contending for? The souls, the lives and the futures of the upcoming generations. Today's educational system had drastically separated from what God first established in this nation through leaders who sought His counsel. The Word of God once served as the basic element in educating Americans. The Ten Commandments were even displayed in schools as a guide to moral attitude and conduct. The state of our educational system may look hopeless, but when something looks hopeless, it is evidence of a spiritual problem. Hope can begin to work in these circumstances. Hope is a spiritual force which grows stronger and stronger the longer we stand. Faith can begin to work in these circumstances. "Now faith is the substance of things, hoped for, the evidence of things not seen" (Hebrews 11:1). Patience can begin to work in these circumstances. The definition of patience is being constant or being the same at all times. As believers exercise these three spiritual forces, the Word of God can work to change the direction of American education. Our

God is a good God! He caused the captivity of Judah and Israel to be reversed, then rebuilt them as they were at first (Jeremiah 33:7). He can do the same in our schools. Pray this prayer of faith and set yourself in agreement with the Word of God for the restoration of God's principles in all levels of education.

"Almighty God, I set myself in agreement with the Word of God and with what You once established in American education. I release my hope and faith in your Word. I patiently expect Your Glory to be manifest in schools across our nation. I come before You on behalf of the students, educators, and administrators of the entire educational system in America. Lord

Jesus, I ask you to restore honor, integrity, virtue, and peace in American classrooms. I confess Isaiah 54:13. 'All thy children shall be taught of the Lord; and great shall be the peace of thy children. Every time I hear a report of violence and term in our schools, I will say out loud, "Our children are taught of the Lord and great is the peace and the Anointing upon them!" Jesus, You and I know the educators and the administrators cannot teach and run our schools without You and Your Anointing. So, I intercede and give thanks for those You have ordained and placed in positions of authority and responsibility in our schools across America. I believe for Your Anointing to be in them and upon them.

I am not waiting until I see the Spirit of God moving in this situation. I am starting my confession NOW! I combine my faith with those who are praying and believing for the wisdom, and honor, power, and Glory of God to be demonstrated in our school system. I am releasing my faith for the next generation! LORD Jesus, I thank You for the redemptive work You are doing in our schools and in the people who run them.

The students and teachers are on Your heart, and they are on mine, too. Our schools will be a joy, and a praise before all the nations of the earth! Nations will fear God and tremble because of all the goodness, peace, prosperity, security and stability You have provided in Jesus! "

*National Center for Education Statistics Report, May 1996

Chapter 10:

A Prayer for Revival

Waves of revival have swept around the world in the Century. Today, the five largest churches in the world are Spirit-filled and growing daily. Pentecostals are increasing in great numbers as worldwide revival brings the life of God to the church and to all mankind. The Hebrew word for revive is chayah which means to live, have life, remain alive, sustain life, nourish, and preserve life, live prosperously, live forever'; be quickened, be alive, be restored to life and health.

According to that definition, revival is not just a one-time shot of life. Revival is a continual nourishment, preservation, quickening and restoration to life. Revival begins when people return to God. It breaks forth from intercessory prayer and continues when people repent and no longer tolerate sin in their lives.

After Jesus ascended to heaven, the disciples returned to the upper room and continued in daily prayer, in one accord, and in one place. Then, at the appointed time, the Holy Spirit burst onto the scene with the sound of a mighty rushing wind. Peter and the others received God's long-awaited promise of the Holy Spirit's anointing. Acts 2:17-19 repeats the prophecy of Joel, "And it shall come to pass in the last days, says God, that I will pour out my spirit in those days, and they shall prophesy... I will show wonders in heaven above and signs in the earth beneath... " (New King James Version).

As they moved out into the streets from the upper room, men from every part of the world saw and heard something different. Peter's great sermon, preached under the anointing of God, brought understanding, conviction of sin and the life of God to those who heard and responded in faith. Prayer, the anointed preaching of the Word, and a supernatural move of God all working together brought revival-God's life-giving power. Oh, what a time to live in! Destruction and despair may be on one hand, but revival and miracles are on the other. Revival is spontaneous and ongoing. It happens when the Spirit of God moves among the people. God never intended for the Pentecostal revival to stop. That is why it is so important to be ready and available as God moves and pours our His Spirit. He can minister life at any moment, to one or to a multitude, to a person in a barren wilderness or to many people in a crowded city.

Revival happens whenever the Word of God prevails. Miracles, signs, and wonders happen wherever the Word of God prevails.

Hearts and lives are changed wherever the Word of God prevails. The Bible says ...God working with them and confirming His word with signs following (Mark 16:20).

Look in the Word of God, which is life to them, revival will come and remain. Revival will become an ongoing way of life. As you set yourself in agreement with Gods will for revival, pray the following prayer or one similar, expecting God to move.

"Father God, because you care for Your people and want all mankind to have life, you desire revival. Your revival brings life and nourishment, preservation, and restoration.

Thank you for sending Jesus to give us Your abundant life Lord, start a

revival in me first. I am Your servant and I place myself in position to receive revival. I feed on the Scriptures as a sheep feed in green pastures, because Your words are life to me.

Holy Spirit of God, you raised Jesus from the dead and You dwell in me. So, I yield to You to energize my spirit, restore my soul, and rejuvenate my mortal body. I renew my mind with Your Word. In my innermost being is a well of living water and I am revived! Revival not only is life to me, but life to everyone who calls on the Name of the Lord. Therefore, I intercede on behalf of the people. I call upon You as the

God of Abraham, Isaac, and Jacob I call upon the mighty Name of Jesus. All of mankind needs life, Lord! All of mankind needs revival because it is life- Your life.

I speak and sow seeds of revival everywhere I go. I send forth angels to reap the harvest of revival all over the world. I put my hand to the sickle to reap the rich harvest of revival in my home, my church, my community, in the marketplace, on the job, in my country and in all the world. Pour Yourself out on the people. Lord of the harvest, send forth laborers, positioning them in strategic places to minister as You pour out Your Spirit on all flesh. Almighty God, show Yourself mighty and strong with signs and wonders. Holy Spirit, breathe on all the people of the world. I pray this in the Name above all names, Jesus. Amen. "

Prayer references:

John 3:16-17

16 For God so loved the world, that he gave his only begotten Son, that whosoever believeth in him should not perish, but have everlasting life. 17 For God sent not his Son into the world to condemn the world; but that the world through him might be saved.

John 10:10

10 The thief cometh not, but for to steal, and to kill, and to destroy: I am come that they might

have life, and that they might have it more abundantly.

Proverbs 4:20-22

20 My son, attend to my words; incline thine ear unto my sayings. 21 Let them not depart from thine eyes; keep them in the midst of thine heart. 22 For they are life unto those that find them, and health to all their flesh.

John 6:63

63 It is the spirit that quickeneth; the flesh profiteth nothing: the words that I speak unto you, they are spirit, and they are life.

Romans 8:11

11 But if the Spirit of him that raised up Jesus from the dead dwell in you, he that raised up Christ from the dead shall also quicken your mortal bodies by his Spirit that dwelleth in you.

Ephesians 4:23-24

23 And be renewed in the spirit of your mind;

24 And that ye put on the new man, which after God is created in righteousness and true holiness.

Colossians 3:10

10 And have put on the new man, which is renewed in knowledge after the image of him that created him:

John 4:14

14 But whosoever drinketh of the water that I shall give him shall never thirst; but the water that I shall give him shall be in him a well of water springing up into everlasting life.

John 7:38

38 He that believeth on me, as the scripture hath said, out of his belly shall flow rivers of living water.

Matthew 13:39

39 The enemy that sowed them is the devil; the harvest is the end of the world; and the reapers are the angels.

Matthew 9:38

38 Pray ye therefore the Lord of the harvest, that he will send forth labourers into his harvest.

II Chronicles 16:9

9 For the eyes of the Lord run to and fro throughout the whole earth, to shew himself strong in the behalf of them whose heart is perfect toward him. Herein thou hast done foolishly: therefore from henceforth thou shalt have wars.

Romans 15:19

19 Through mighty signs and wonders, by the power of the Spirit of God; so that from Jerusalem, and round about unto Illyricum, I have fully preached the gospel of Christ.

Chapter Eleven:

Understanding Redemption

God can establish each of us in the faith according to the plan of redemption which had been hidden over the ages. After the Fall in the Garden of Eden, God spoke and outlined his plan. His plan put Satan out of business completely. God has commanded that his plan of redemption be revealed to His people through His word. This outline will help you, step by step, and you will be able to understand the reality of it and prevent Satan from lording over you.

1. The plan of redemption called for an Incarnation (The Union of divinity with Humanity in Jesus Christ).

    Man was the key figure in the fall. Hence, why it took a man, Jesus, to be the key figure in the redemption of mankind. When we were born in this world, ruled by Satan, we didn't naturally know who God was. Therefore, the whole purpose of incarnation is that men may be given the right to become sons of God by receiving the nature of God (John 1: 12-13 12 But as many as received him, to them gave he power to become the sons of God, even to them that believe on his name: 13 Which were born, not of blood, nor of the will of the flesh, nor of the will of man, but of God.; II Peter 1:3-4; 3 According as his divine power hath given unto us all things that pertain unto life and godliness, through the knowledge of him that hath called us to glory and virtue: 4 Whereby are given unto us exceeding great and precious promises: that by these ye might be partakers of the divine nature, having escaped the corruption that is in the world through lust.).

2. Redemption comes from knowledge.

God's divine power has already given us everything that we need to pertain to life and godliness. You can escape the corruption in this world and take hold of the divine nature of God. Through it you can have peace and grace many times over through the knowledge of God and of Jesus our Lord (I Peter 1:1-4; 1 Peter, an apostle of Jesus Christ, to the strangers scattered throughout Pontus, Galatia, Cappadocia, Asia, and Bithynia, 2 Elect according to the foreknowledge of God the Father, through sanctification of the Spirit, unto obedience and sprinkling of the blood of Jesus Christ: Grace unto you, and peace, be multiplied. 3 Blessed be the God and Father of our Lord Jesus Christ, which according to his abundant mercy hath begotten us again unto a lively hope by the resurrection of Jesus Christ from the dead, 4 To an inheritance incorruptible, and undefiled, and that fadeth not away, reserved in heaven for you,). It is there for you. However, this revelation knowledge is not a sense knowledge, doctrine, philosophies, and creeds. It is the real reality and full of truth of the word of God, which is revealed by the Holy Spirit (James 3:13-18; 13 Who is a wise man and endued with knowledge among you? let him shew out of a good conversation his works with meekness of wisdom. 14 But if ye have bitter envying and strife in your hearts, glory not, and lie not against the truth. 15 This wisdom descendeth not from above, but is earthly, sensual, devilish. 16 For where envying and strife is, there is confusion and every evil work. 17 But the wisdom that is from above is first pure, then peaceable, gentle, and easy to be intreated, full of mercy and good fruits, without partiality, and without hypocrisy. 18 And the fruit of righteousness is sown in peace of them that make peace.).

Revelation knowledge is literally knowledge that is brought to you by revelation.

3. Satan's lordship has been broken.

Revelation 12:11 says that believers overcome by the blood of the lamb and by the word of their testimony, or confession. Confession brings us into possession. You have to boldly confess, " I am an overcomer by the blood of the Lamb and by the word of my testimony. I am redeemed from the lordship of Satan. I can stop his assignments every time." (II Corinthians 10:4; 4 (For the weapons of our warfare are not carnal, but mighty through God to the pulling down of strong holds; James 4:7; 7 Submit yourselves therefore to God. Resist the devil, and he will flee from you.) Satan is not the head of the Church. Jesus is the Head of the

Church (Ephesians 4:15-16; 15 But speaking the truth in love, may grow up into him in all things, which is the head, even Christ: 16 From whom the whole body fitly joined together and compacted by that which every joint supplieth, according to the effectual working in the measure of every part, maketh increase of the body unto the edifying of itself in love. Ephesians 5:23; 23 For the husband is the head of the wife, even as Christ is the head of the church: and he is the saviour of the body. Colossians 1:18 18 And he is the head of the body, the church: who is the beginning, the firstborn from the dead; that in all things he might have the preeminence; Colossians 2:10; 10 And ye are complete in him, which is the head of all principality and power:) Satan has no rule over you.

4. You are brought with a price.

I Corinthians says that we are the temple of the Holy Spirit, which is received from God. Simply put, we don't own ourselves. Through the plan of redemption, we were bought with a price paid. Because of that price paid, we should glorify God in our bodies and spirits.

5. God's response

When you begin to take hold of your place and assume your rights and privileges in Christ, then this is where God will begin to respond to you. Our inheritance can be seen in the word of God (Acts 20:32; 32 And now, brethren, I commend you to God, and to the word of his grace, which is able to build you up, and to give you an inheritance among all them which are sanctified; Colossians 1:12; 12 Giving thanks unto the Father, which hath made us meet to be partakers of the inheritance of the saints in light:) As you are studying the scripture in this outline, our prayer is that you will come to the full knowledge of who you are in Christ, especially in the light of the redemption plan.

Chapter Twelve:

Understanding Confessions

The words that we speak are spiritual, they have power. Each word that we speak is important to our lives. Jesus said, I say unto you, that every idle word that men shall speak, they shall give account thereof in the day of judgment. For by thy words, thou shall be justified, and by thy words thou shall be condemned" (Matthew 12:36-37).

When God created the human race, He placed in us the special ability to choose our own words and speak them forth at will. That ability that he gave, makes the human being different from all the other creatures, even the angels. Angels can speak but they can only speak the words Gods tell them to speak. They act, but only by the command of God.

Man has the unique ability to choose and speak words, this has become a key factor in the development of the human race. Proverbs 12:14 says that we shall be satisfied with good by the fruit of our mouths. In Matthew 12;34, Jesus says, "out of the abundance of the heart the mouth speaketh."

If we are not enjoying the reality of God's word, then it is because of our confessions have us bound. Confessing the word of God isn't lying, we must realize that we are not trying to get God to do anything. The benefits God has given us in His word are ours already and Satan is trying to steal them.

So, confessing isn't lying. It's a statement of truth. If you didn't know Jesus bore your sickness and disease and told someone you were healed because the bible says, "by His stripes you were healed," is speaking the truth that Jesus has already redeemed you from the curse of the law (Deuteronomy 28; Galatians 3:13).

Here are five basics confessions for you to use so that you can enjoy all that God has for you:

1. Jesus is my Lord Philippians 2:9-11

"I confess the complete lordship of Jesus Christ. Jesus is LORD over all, and He has given me authority. As I confess Him, His Word and His Name, and resist Satan in His

Name, Satan must bow His knee."

2. I don't have a care. I Peter 5:7; Psalms 37: 23-24

"I cast all my care on Jesus because He cares for me. He upholds me as He guides my steps."

3. I do not want. Psalms 23:1; Philippians 4:19

"The Lord is my Shepherd. I shall not want. For my God supplies all my need according to His riches in glory by Christ Jesus.

4. I am free from sin, sickness, sorrow, grief, and fear. Isaiah 53:3-5; Matthew 8:17; I Peter 2:24

"Every sin, sickness, disease, sorrow and grief was laid on Jesus so that I could be free from them. Therefore, today I am forgiven, healed, healthy and well. I live in divine

health "

5. Jesus is made unto us Wisdom, righteousness, sanctification and redemption.

I Corinthians 1:30; Colossians 2:10

"I confess that Jesus is my wisdom, righteousness, sanctification, and redemption. Only in Him am I entirely complete."

If you want to change your circumstances, fill your heart with the word of God. Confess these truths and other scriptures so that the words that come out of your mouth are life-changing words. Let's say what the word of God says.

Chapter Thirteen:

YOUR OPPORTUNITY TO PARTNER

We are seeing that partnership is indeed dynamic. But partnership is not a one-sided relationship. As the Apostle Paul said, "I thank my God upon every remembrance of you... For your fellowship in the gospel from the first day until now... because I have you in my heart; inasmuch as both in my bonds, and in the defense and confirmation of the gospel, ye are all partakers of my grace (Philippians 1:3, 5,7)." Paul was saying "1 have you in my heart, I'm praying for you and I'm not going to let you fail!" His partners had become a major part of his ministry. They fought alongside him in prayer, they ministered to his needs, and provided for other ministers that he sent to help build them spiritually. That's how partnership works.

The Partners have a significant role in this ministry. God provides for the ministry through them- through their prayers, words of encouragement and support, and through their giving to what God is doing through the ministry. And every day we see and hear of the great rewards they are receiving as a result of their partnership. If God is directing you to become a Partner, or if you are already a Partner, press in to get a revelation of God's will for you, and then get ready for the adventure and rewards that come when you release the power of partnership in your life.

Chapter fourteen:

The Blessing of the Twice Sown Seed

"And he...took the five loaves, and two fishes, and looking up toward heaven he blessed, and brake, and gave the loaves to his disciples, and the disciples to the multitude. And they did all eat and were filled: and they took up of the fragments that remained twelve baskets full. And they that had eaten were about five thousand men beside women and children " (Matthew 14:19-21).

Sowing into Tiffany Long Ministries stretches further than the hundreds of lives you can touch. It stretches from orphanages to healing ministries to evangelical meetings to medical teams. We reach all over the globe through the principle of the twice sown-seed.

When you give to Tiffany Long Ministries, 10 percent of every gift is given to other ministries that reach people we can't. We actually re-sow a tenth of your gift and product purchase into lives all over the world. And just like the boy who gave his loaves and fish to Jesus, we see the increase on the seed-faith gifts of our partners. Through partnership in ministry, we are reaching greater numbers of people than any of us could reach on our own- people who have no other way to hear the good news.

We stand with ministries which train and minister through educating, credentialing, and assisting men and women in the Word of God, prayer, and divine leadership. We support outreaches which conduct yearly ministerial conferences in several countries, providing Bibles in English and other native languages to equip Pastors to win the lost to Christ...a tremendous need! Providing theological training and books for Pastors and ministers, developing Bible schools, helping the children, feeding the poor, promoting soul winning and reaching the lost and church planting. We promote the gospel through broadcasting Gospel and Christian music as well as local, national, and international ministers. We give into other ministries that teach local ministers by the hundreds every year in Guatemala, send evangelistic teams into the isolated Islands and mountains of the Philippines, and telecast the good news across Eastern Europe.

In addition, we support locally with our children's ministries, volunteer services programs, campus and young adult outreach, medical assistance, job creation, evangelism, continuing education assistance, clothing, food, teaching and preaching. You enable us to put legs to our prayers by putting substance into our hands to be effective soldiers of the cross. As a result, you will share the reward of this harvest someday! Lives are changed Eternally.

Blessings overflow to the giver. That's the power of partnership. That's the power of the twice-sown-seed!

A PARTNER...........

One who shares responsibility in some common activity with another individual or group.

Our Responsibility:

- Pray on a daily basis that God's blessing be upon you.

Provide spiritual and life enrichment resources for you online.

- Bless you with a free gift from time to time (such as music or message downloads or other gifts)
- Provide partner conferences, meetings, and events online and offline
- Serve Christ through serving mankind.
- Provide you with a tuition paid course through Interfaith University (Optional)

Your Responsibility:

- Pray for us always.
- Support our outreach efforts especially in your area

- Prayerfully sow financially into our outreach efforts.
- Always uplift us with the words that you speak.
- Serve Christ through serving mankind.

Tiffany Long, I want to access the Power of this anointed Prayer Partnership!

My Name is:

_____

_____

My Address is:

_____

Phone:

_____

_____

I am writing my prayer request on this form.

Enclosed is my love gift of $

    I am pledging _ $7 _$IO _$20 _$100 _$500 _Other $ per month to help you accomplish the vision of winning the lost and encouraging the saints through the Word of God!

Signature:

_____

_____

Prayer Request-

Chapter Fifteen:

PRAYER FOR MINISTRY PARTNERS

Father, in the Name of Jesus, we pray to you on behalf of our all of our partners, who pray for us, support our local meetings, sow financially into this ministry, and always uplift the ministry, our Pastors and their family with the words that they speak.

Father, we thank you for our partners and for their service and dedication to serve you. Thank you that they bring forth the fruit of the Spirit: love, joy, peace, longsuffering, gentleness, goodness, faith, meekness, and temperance.

Father, thank you that our partners are good ground, that they hear Your Word and understand it, and that the Word bears fruit in their lives. They are like trees planted by rivers of water that bring forth fruit in its season. Their leaf shall not wither, and whatever they do shall prosper.

From the first day we heard of our partners, we have not stopped praying for them, asking God to give them wise minds and spirits attuned to his will, and so acquire a thorough understanding of the ways in which God works. Our partners are merciful as our Father is merciful. They will judge only as they want to be judged. They do not condemn, and they are not condemned. Our partners forgive others and people forgive them. They give and men will give to them- yes, good measure, pressed down, shaken together, running over will they pour into their laps for whatever measure they use with other people, they will use in their dealings with them.

Father, we ask you to bless our partners with all spiritual blessings in heavenly places that good will might come to them. They are generous and lend freely. They conduct their affairs with justice. Lord, Your Word says that surely, they will never be shaken. They are righteous men and women who will be remembered forever. They will have no fear of bad news; their hearts are steadfast, trusting in you.

Lord, we ask that your plans be fulfilled in their lives, and we thank you for your mercies on their behalf. In Jesus' name we pray. Amen.

Colossians 1:9 For this cause we also, since the day we heard it, do not cease to pray for you, and to desire that ye might be filled with the knowledge of his will in all wisdom and spiritual understanding.

Psalm 112:5-9 [5] A good man sheweth favour, and lendeth: he will guide his affairs with discretion. [6] Surely, he shall not be moved for ever: the righteous shall be in everlasting remembrance. [7] He shall not be afraid of evil tidings: his heart is fixed, trusting in the Lord. **8** His heart is established, he shall not be afraid, until he see his desire upon his enemies. **9** He hath dispersed, he hath given to the poor; his righteousness endureth for ever; his horn shall be exalted with honour.

Jeremiah 29:11 For I know the thoughts that I think toward you, saith the Lord, thoughts of peace, and not of evil, to give you an expected end.

About The Author

Tiffany Long was born and raised in sweet home Alabama. She graduated from Highschool at the age of 16 with honors and went on to attend college where she studied communications where she was an honor student. Communications is something that she has a passion for. She wants to show others the power of their voice and how they can use their voice to proclaim what God says so they can see the desired results in their everyday lives.

www.tlongbooks.com

Made in the USA
Columbia, SC
25 May 2024